THIS BOOK BELONGS TO

____

____

____

ISBN: 9798564902656
Imprint: Independently published

PRANAB PUBLISHING

The gift of love.
The gift of peace. ...

Coloring Book

The other women left, but Mary Magdalene remained.
Jesus appeared to her.

Jesus Heals a Man Born Blind